A Special
GIFT

Presented to:

_____

From:

_____

Date:

_____

Published by C.R. Gibson®

C.R. Gibson® is a registered trademark of Thomas Nelson, Inc., Nashville, Tennessee 37214

Designed by Anderson Thomas Design, Nashville, Tennessee

Written and developed by Matthew A. Price

Printed in Mexico

GB110

ISBN 0-7667-8194-1

UPC 0-82272-47844-2

MAY YOU FIND
SERENITY
*Expressions and Words
of Sympathy and Comfort*

C.R.Gibson®
FINE GIFTS SINCE 1870

*S*oft as the voice of an angel,
Breathing a lesson unheard,
Hope with a gentle persuasion,
Whispers her comforting word:
Wait 'til the darkness is over,
Wait 'til the tempest is done,
Hope for the sunshine tomorrow,
After the shower is gone.

—ALICE HAWTHORNE

There is no easy way to overcome sorrow, to neatly fill the void carved out by a personal and emotional loss. Kind words, thoughtful gestures, quiet support – all of these loving expressions are welcome balm for the broken hearted. Yet only time and an abiding faith will begin to heal a grieving spirit.

*M*emories and hope are the emotional bookends of adjusting to a world that has been dimmed by sadness and uncertainty. Reflect on times of joy – days you hoped would stretch out forever, hours that drifted away like clouds on a breezy afternoon. These moments cannot be relived but they can be recaptured. And the memory of yesterday can prepare you for a warmer and brighter tomorrow, a time when happier memories can be created.

*L*earn what you can from this time. Wisdom is born of adversity and a day will come when you will provide solace to another, when you will stand as a pillar of strength, when you will be able to speak with words of comfort that can only come from experience.

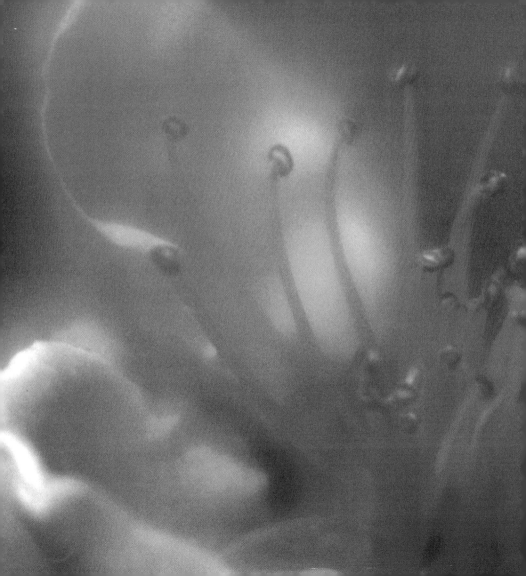

You are a person of character. Resolution, fortitude, and strength are what defines you. But don't be hesitant to reach out to others for support. Don't forget that there are many, many people who care about you and will not let you forget that you are part of an extended family – a family that is built on friendship and love.

Angels descending, bringing from above,
Echoes of mercy, whispers of love. —FANNY CROSBY

A Scrapbook of

Memories

A time will come when you will want to look back on this period, to recall your thoughts as you journeyed along this emotional valley. When you are ready, jot down a few of these feelings . . .

_____

_____

_____

_____

_____

_____

_____

_____

_____

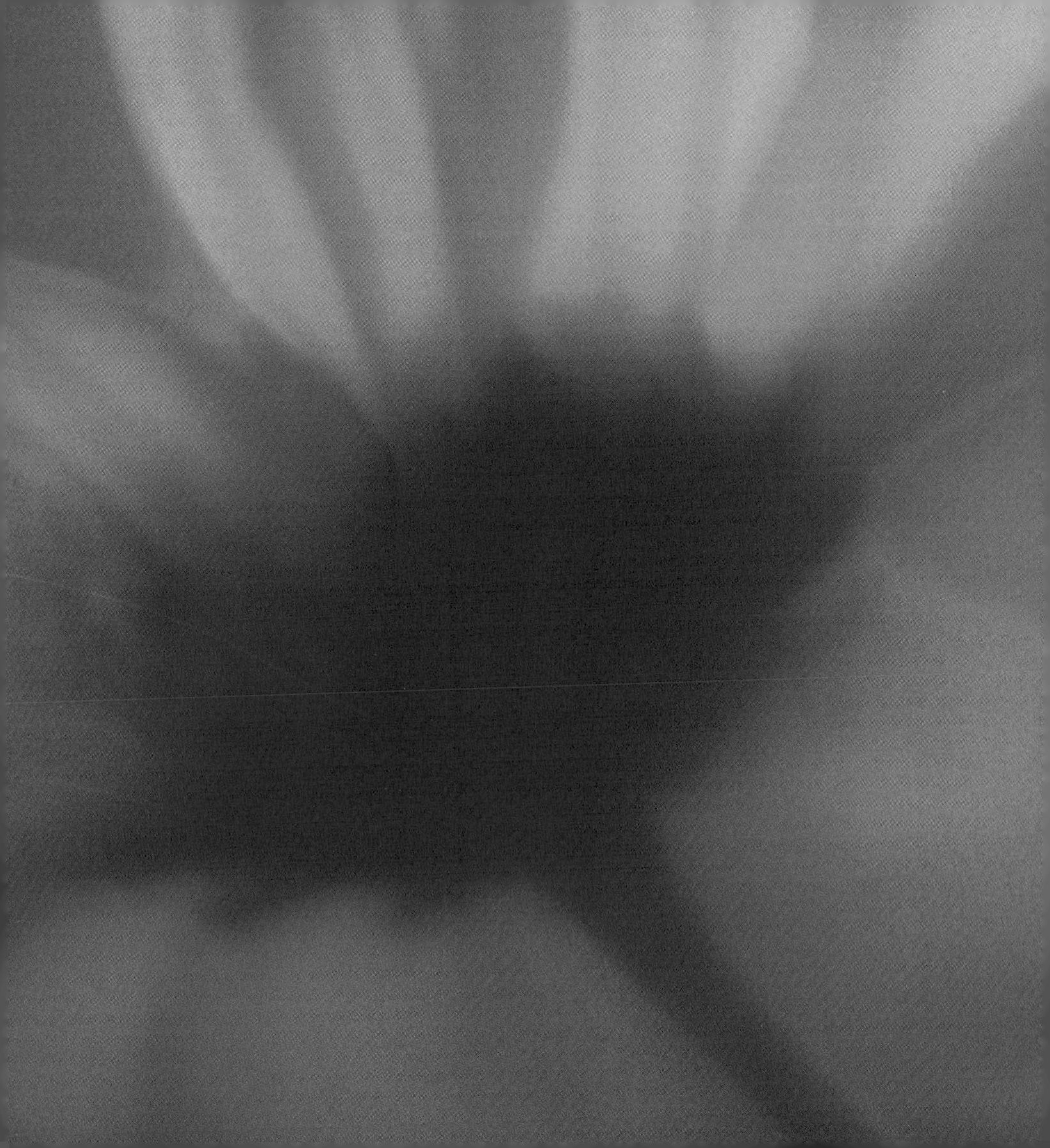

Have Hope

Though clouds environ 'round
And gladness hides her face in scorn,
Put off the shadow from thy brow;
No night but hath its morn.

—FRIEDRICH VON SCHILLER

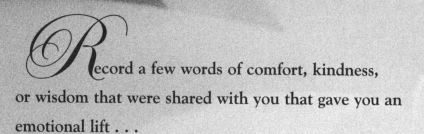

*R*ecord a few words of comfort, kindness, or wisdom that were shared with you that gave you an emotional lift . . .

_____

_____

_____

_____

_____

_____

_____

_____

_____

*I*n heaven above,
And earth below,
    They best can serve true gladness,
Who meet most feelingly the calls of sadness.

—William Wordsworth

ote a poem, a story, an anecdote, or an article
that brought comfort or inspiration . . .

Grace comes into the soul, as the morning

sun into the world; first a dawning; then a light;

and at last the sun in its full and excellent brightness.

—Thomas Adams

$\mathscr{L}$ist any special cards, gifts, flowers, or phone calls you have received . . .

_____

_____

_____

_____

_____

_____

_____

_____

_____

_____

_____

*W*hen the spent sun throws up its rays on cloud
And goes down burning into the gulf below,
No voice in nature is heard to cry aloud
At what has happened . . .

. . . Birds, at least, must know

It is the change to darkness in the sky.

Murmuring something quiet in her breast,

One bird begins to close a faded eye;

Or overtaken too far from her nest,

Hurrying low above the grove, some waif

Swoops just in time to her remembered tree . . .

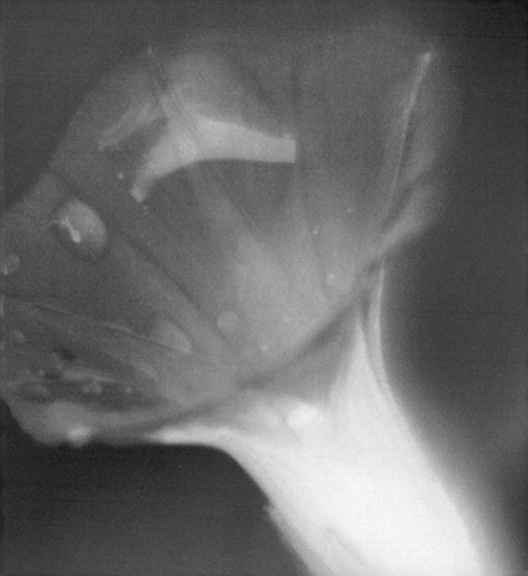

*A*t most she thinks or twitters softly, "Safe!"

Now let the night be dark for all of me.

Let the night be too dark for me to see

Into the future. Let what will be, be.

—Robert Frost

*T*hat all the jarring notes of life,

Seem blending in a psalm;

And all the angles of its strife,

Slow rounding into calm.

And so the shadows fall apart,

And so the west-winds play;

And all the windows of my heart,

I open to the day.

—John Greenleaf Whittier

MAY YOU FIND
SERENITY